Pickled Pieces and Rollicking Rhymes

I0586850

Jim Connelly

Other Books by Jim Connelly

Tom and Anna on the Trail: the Case of the Missing Schoolgirl (2014)

Tom and Anna in Danger: the Case of the Disappearing Dogs (2014)

Tom and Anna take a Chance: the Case of the Bungling Bird Bandits (2015)

My Folk: Four Hundred Years of Hazards, Tooths, and Connellys (2015)

Mountain Boy (2016)

Talk of the Town: Warragul/Drouin (2017)

Talk of the Town (2): Warragul/Drouin (2018)

Pickled Pieces and Rollicking Rhymes

Copyright

A CIP catalogue record for this book is available from the National Library of Australia

First published in Australia 2019

James Timothy Connelly

12 Craig Street

Warragul, Victoria, Australia.

ajcon@dcsi.net.au

For Anne

Cover design by Craig Braithwaite, aussiepics

If you get too serious you could die of starch

(Cyndi Lauper)

A Thorny Issue

I do appreciate the little things our Shire Council does for us here in Warragul. You know, the little things that don't get much publicity, like providing blackberries for passers-by. Those blackberries, they're the icing on the cake. You find them all over the place – outside the State School, at the bottom end of Bowen Street, along the Linear Trail. The walk from the bowling green to the shops in Warragul could well be named, 'Blackberry Avenue'. And very fine blackberries they are, too. Come summer, those swelling berries will be in full fruiting, crushing lusciously on the palate. But why not elsewhere? The Shire's garden staff could easily plant out our grass verges with blackberries along the main roads of the town. Newcomers to the district could be presented with a bundle of blackberry plants as a welcoming gift. Warragul could become known as the Blackberry Capital of Gippsland. We'd drive into town amidst the waving fronds of blackberries. Rabbits could be brought in to live in them, to delight the little ones. Snakes, too, could be part of the attraction, and foxes. Blackberry pie would become our distinctive local delicacy, like pumpkin pie in Queensland. I'll vote for anyone who runs for Council on a blackberry ticket.

99.967 km

Now we know just how far we are from somewhere. If you go to the overhead bridge at the railway station in Warragul, you'll see a sign attached to it on the Queen Street side of the bridge. It says: *'99.967 kilometres'.* Where to? Where from? It doesn't say. No clues given, but we're smart enough to know that it must mean that distance from Melbourne. Not 100 kilometres. Not 99 and a half kilometres. 99.967 kilometres, exactly. I have a picture in my mind of two men carrying a ten-metre measuring chain, marking the distance, starting at Flinders Street station and continuing through rain, hail, heat, and tempest, over the months until they got to HERE, and the distance was 99.967 kilometres from where they started. Sadly, we lack that precision of mind of those early railway men. Why, it isn't twenty-two kilometres from Drouin to Neerim South. No, it's 21.854 kilometres. This lack of precision will one day be the ruin of us. We must teach our children to be precise. Hammer it home. Would that we could get those railway men back. The ones who put that sign on the bridge. We could get them to run the town for a full week – or 10,080 minutes to be precise!

The Used Car Market

Have you ever tried to sell your car? Not traded it in. Sold it on the open market. There's the first fallacy. There *is* no open market. It's all a done deal – there's a gigantic conspiracy to offer cars for sale at vastly inflated prices and to offer to buy cars at miserable figures that would make even Ned Kelly blush. These reflections follow my attempts to sell my beloved 2003 Mitsubishi Magna. It had served me well for many a year, and I was deeply attached to it. It had its faults. Actually only one. It was prone to run into gateposts and concrete walls at shopping centres. So it was both battered and beloved. But it had to go. It had taken to sitting in the garage, unused, for months on end, quietly running down its battery and gathering dust. My first gambit was to advertise it in the local paper, which brought one nibble, but no bite. Offended by the public's failure to recognise its true worth, I decided to leave it where it was. Let it gather dust and run down its battery, and live in decrepit isolation like Miss Faversham. Then, out of the blue, a Prince Charming appeared. How discerning he was. He thought the car was beautiful. Yes, I'll buy it, he said, with a premium for your personal loss. Ah, what a man! What a car!

Up in the Air

I flew to Perth recently – and back. Like many things, flying is better in the prospect than in the actuality. How marvellous to sweep through the skies, beyond all mundane cares and responsibilities, whisked, almost instantly, to fabled places far away. Now the actuality. You get up at the crack of dawn to be at the airport two hours before your flight leaves. You're treated to a security examination that spares no indignity. There's a two-hour delay because your cabin crew are stuck on an incoming flight that is itself delayed. This at least gives you time to examine your fellow-passengers, most of whom look like terrorists. At last the boarding call comes, and you take your place, imprisoned in the serried ranks of sardines, far from the aisle, far from the window, far from hope if the worst happens. The engines roar, the plane shakes. How can these pieces of aluminium riveted together by fallible human hands survive this punishment? Now you're in the air, beyond all rescue. The plane banks at an angle more than the laws of physics will allow. There's a maniac in control! But, no, the plane settles down. And here comes that nice stewardess with a cardboard box of delightful airline fare. All is well, all serene. Ah, this is the life!

Destruction and Dollars

There's a man called Banksy. Or a woman called Banksy. No-one knows. He (or she) lives his (or her) life in anonymity. But he (or she) paints, and sells their paintings for large sums of money, call it millions of dollars. Last year, did you hear, one of his (or her) paintings was sold at auction for $1.8 million, but at the third fall of the hammer, half of it disintegrated. It wasn't reported whether Banksy himself (or herself) also disintegrated, but he or she disappeared (if they were there) into their secret world. The painting has now gone up in value, they say, what's left of it. It's given me ideas. I'm always searching for ways to make a quiet million or two. I could sell my books with half the pages not stuck in, so that they fall out in the hands of the buyer. The books would then be worth more. Or I could simply sell the books with half the pages missing in the first place – and charge double. Maybe I could sell the books at auction, and arrange that they burst into flames the instant they are bought. The charred remains would, on the same principle, be worth more than the original selling price. The ultimate would be to change my name and lose myself, like Banksy, in the crowd. I've thought about it. I could call myself 'Hanksy-Panksy'.

The Pleasures of Cruising

My wife is going on about us taking a cruise. She cuts the ads out of the paper and surreptitiously places them under my pillow. Her theory is that even if I don't read them, the contents will seep into my brain through a process of telepathic osmosis. I'm not keen on cruising. I try to reason with her. We debate the matter. Her arguments in favour are (i) no dishwashing, and (ii) no packing up each day. My arguments cover such ground as sea-sickness, ship-wide pandemics, falling overboard, having to talk to people, bad weather, and not getting the crosswords in the daily paper. Besides, I've seen photos of the live-sheep exporting ships, and it seems to me that life cruising the ocean must be something the same. Could I stand it? There's no escape once you go up that gangplank. Just like the sheep. I might go mad. I imagine the headlines, *'Crazed Man Attacks Cruise Captain In Indian Ocean.* My attitude to deep-sea voyaging has been fashioned by 'Moby Dick'. How many more white whales are out there, lurking, waiting to attack? They sneak up from behind, you know. Or come at you out of the sun. No, cruising is not for me. I like to stay at home in my own comfortable bed, even if my pillow has been infiltrated by agents spreading false propaganda.

Threats to Life

Dorothea McKellar set my alarm bells ringing when I was in Grade 6, with that talk of droughts and flooding rains. I thought Gippsland would be safe from these perils, but I found out differently. There are tiger snakes lurking behind the lilli-pillies, and red-back spiders behind the bathroom door. Why, a woman was seriously injured in a kangaroo attack the other day. Those kangaroos. I've never trusted them. But now there's another threat to my peace of mind. Gippsland, those seismologists are saying, is one of the most earthquake-prone regions in Australia. I can't sleep at night. Earthquakes happen more at night, you know. I lie awake thinking of those tectonic plates, grinding against each other, planning another slippage. There was the big Moe earthquake in 2012. Just long enough ago for us to relax. That's how they work. They lull you into a sense of being safe, then – SHAZOOM! – they rip against each other one dark night and set the earth shaking and buildings crumbling. And do you think those insurance companies will take you seriously? 'Act of God', they call them, these earthquakes. Leave God out of it, I say, as I pull the blankets over my head, and pray that that earthquake doesn't come tonight.

Long-distance Motoring

I remember when the Hume Highway was single-lane all the way to Sydney. You got a truck in front of you and followed it until it ran out of petrol. Now it's two-lane, divided highway all the way. You put your car on cruise control outside Sydney and leave it there until you reach Melbourne seven hours later. That's the theory. The truth is, first, your wife insists you change drivers every hour. That loses one hour in total. The next thing, you pull in to a service centre for some over-priced petrol and some under-cooked food. Another hour gone. You must stop at the dog-on-the-tucker-box for old times' sake. Forty-five minutes. What about the submarine at Holbrook? Must see it again. And isn't there a garden centre in Holbrook for that banana passionfruit someone's been looking for? No, there isn't a garden centre in Holbrook, though it takes thirty minutes to find that out. You cross the Murray and the air becomes strangely purer. There's one more place to see. Chiltern. Famous for Barrie Cassidy and the world's biggest vine. The vine is there, but Barrie Cassidy seems to have gone. It's all downhill now. The Tullamarine, the Burnley Tunnel … and, there, I can see Warragul in the distance. Might get home before midnight.

14

Division of Labour

We've come to some useful working arrangements, my wife and I. For instance, she cooks the meals and I eat them. She makes the bed and I lie on it. One of these arrangements is that she looks after the flower garden and I see to the vegetables. You should see the flowers. It's like the Garden of Eden. The Floriade come to a back garden in Warragul. Costa should bring his team here to film them. On the other side of the lawn lie the vegetable beds. Ah me! What heroic efforts have occurred here! What powerful strokes of the spade! What smooth thrusts of the hoe! What tender murmurings at planting time! But, I ask you, why does it take so long for potatoes to grow? Or carrots? Can't they produce instant carrot seed in this enlightened age? And what is it with those weeds? We can send a man to the moon, but we can't keep weeds out of our garden. What are our research institutions doing, for goodness sake? And as for those gardening books, with their rosy pictures of fat pumpkins and golden ears of corn and luscious green beans spilling over the basket sides, false advertising, I call it. Fake news! Still, there's always hope. I'm negotiating with the powers-that-be to swap. I'll do the flowers next year. They need a man's hand. It's clear.

Sudoku

Don't start. That's my advice. Sudoku is a dangerous addiction. I was led into this wicked pastime by my wife. Not that she talked me into it. I just couldn't stand the smug look on her face when she completed a puzzle, then would look across the table with that faintly contemptuous smirk all husbands know so well. I began, in secret, to dabble in this occult mystery. In secret, because I could never confess my inadequacies to the other side of the table. But now I get the puzzles out all the time, though my aforesaid partner insists I move on from the 'Easy' section to the 'Medium'. Not for me. Winning is my motivation, like the Australian cricket team. Playing the game is secondary. I read about the drugs trial in Sydney that had to be aborted after three months because the jurors were playing Sudoku while they listened to the evidence. Shows you where addiction can lead you. Sudoku has its benefits, though. You do it with numbers, not words, so it's an international sport, and there's no home-ground advantage. They have competitions. One of them is three-dimensional Sudoku, which must be rather like Rubik's Cube. You can download Sudokus from your computer, but, as I warned you, don't do it. Start your first Sudoku, and your number's up!

The Melbourne Cup

I like racehorses. I've even been to the races a few times, but the horses go past in such a blur of colour and speed I have no idea who's won until the numbers are posted when the race is over. You can't hear the course broadcast, and there's no time to look down at your race card. Still there's a surge of adrenalin at that moment, enough, at any rate, to make you stay for the next race. I saw this year's Cup in the comfort of somebody else's lounge room with a small number of others. I put in my two dollars for the sweep with a deep sense of resignation. It's not within living memory that I've won a sweep, raffle, scratch card or lottery of any kind. When I was captain of my cricket team, they sacked me. I lost the toss every time. The race began and ended in the usual blur. While I sat in philosophical contemplation as my horse finished near the tail and someone else scooped up the prize money from the sweep, I worked out the Connelly Law of Diminishing Returns. Your horse's odds multiplied by the age of the jockey will always be greater than the money left in your pocket at the end of the race. I just have to convert that to a betting system to make my pile. I'll keep you posted.

Minding the Kids

'Yes, we'd love to have them for the weekend. Of course'. That's the grandchildren, aged eight and six. Boys. Can you guess where this is leading? We laid our plans. The Park, and the Library figured prominently. But these were all done by five o'clock Friday. What to do next? They were waiting for this, these two. In unison, with hands clasped and upturned eyes: 'Can we watch Kids TV?' We did our best. We appealed to reason; we brought forward health and safety arguments; we quoted parental instructions. But to no avail. Have you ever tried to withstand the psychological pressure of two practised operators? We're only human. So they watched Kids TV and we prepared tea. I won't go into the evening meal in detail. Suffice it to say that there were elements of persuasion, blackmail, reward, and coercion at various stages of the meal. And that over, there was time for a game before bed. 'British Bulldog?' they urged. 'No, a quiet game so you won't get too excited.' So we played draughts. Draughts. Now I'm pretty good at draughts. I smiled confidently as the pieces were set out. The first game took fifteen minutes; the second ten minutes, the third five minutes. I lost them all. '*You* put the kids to bed,' I called to my wife.

The Grand Old Game

I'm a fair-minded man, and like to acknowledge gifts and abilities in everyone I come across. So, although I appreciate that there are many fine players in the game at the moment, it's a remarkable coincidence that the eighteen best footballers playing AFL just now should all play for the one club, Essendon. I once wanted to do a PhD thesis on the Essendon Football Club, but the university authorities denied me. It seems they barrack for Carlton. I read everything I can get my hands on about the Dons. I once bought a book called 'The Red and the Black', only to find it was about nineteenth-century France. Disappointing, but just ask me anything about nineteenth-century France! The team called itself the Bombers in 1940, when the newspapers were all about real bombers. In my infancy I guess I was confused between the two. I've seen the Bombers play many times, mostly in the last quarter. They used to let you in for free after three-quarter time, you know. Tipungwuti is my favourite player; I like his name ... and I saw him play for Drouin once. These days I prepare carefully for every game. I get out my Essendon beanie. I get out my Essendon scarf. I put on my Essendon socks. Then I turn the telly on.

People you Meet

I was walking along Brandy Creek Road with an empty bucket in my hand. I was returning it to a friend. Nevertheless I was feeling goofy about it. I mean, an empty bucket! Then I met a man walking the other way with a glass of white wine in his hand. He had his daughter with him. She also carried a glass of white wine. We tried to explain ourselves to one another. As we parted, I noticed they kept looking back at me. The next day I was in Drouin and met a woman who had a cockatoo on her shoulder. I stopped to ask whether she called it 'Captain Flint' a la Long John Silver. Shortly afterwards, back in Warragul, in the gathering dark of evening, I met a young man walking *backwards* down the round metal railing running alongside the down driveway from the roof of Coles supermarket. There was a precipitous drop on one side. I stood and watched him, partly to be ready to call the ambulance, and partly to congratulate him when he got to the bottom. He did. He says he was practising his *parkour*, which is apparently an urban athletic game played by madmen in France. Maybe we could invent a local game using empty buckets, wine glasses, cockatoos and driveway railings. Madness needn't be confined to France.

Keeping them Honest

Don Chipp, the founder of the Democrats, adopted the slogan, 'Keep the bastards honest'. It worked because it tapped into a deep vein of suspicion of politicians. Some say that suspicion came from our convict days. I was thinking of that slogan when I rolled up to vote at the State elections down in Queen Street in Warragul. I voted early, before the actual polling day, as did half the electorate. It makes you wonder about the money spent on political advertising. It's too late for many people. They've already voted. There was no sense of suspicion and division outside the polling booth. The party faithful were there handing out How-to-Vote cards. A couple of the candidates were there in person, which I gave them a tick for. It was quite a jolly scene there in the street. The hander-outers from each party were chatting together, sharing jokes, even handing out cards for each other if someone had to go away for a toilet break. Why the politicians can't get along the same way, I don't know. Maybe each session of parliament should start with the members going out into Spring Street and having a street party with the passers-by. 'The parliament that plays together stays together' would be the slogan. Don Chipp would like that.

Finding a Wife

The latest census shows that for every hundred people in Baw Baw Shire, 49.3 are males and 50.7 are females. So there should be a fifty-fifty chance of anyone finding a wife or husband. One difficulty for the girls is that it's traditional for the bloke to propose, though letting women do the job every 29th February helps! However, it wasn't like this in the old days. A hundred years and more ago, round here, there were many more men than women. Good pickings for the girls! But, in the fierce competition, the young fellows were at a disadvantage. The more mature blokes had more money, better prospects, and maybe more charm, which often left the younger ones at the barrier when the rope went up. So a lot of women married much older men, while some of the men had to go looking for brides in places far away, like Melbourne. One marriage of a local couple was between a fifty-year-old bridegroom and a twenty-eight-year-old bride. She went on to bear ten children. Another bride of twenty-five summers married a man twelve years older than herself and bore him eleven children. Things have changed. These days the average number of children in a family is 1.8, and as for tying the marriage knot, a lot of couples think they're better off without it!

Spring Cleaning

I rose from the conjugal bed as though called by some external force. An internal force was also calling me – to the bathroom! I glanced at the calendar. 30th November. That's what was calling me. Spring cleaning day. The windows have been the subject of much discussion over the kitchen table. Today is the day for action. Negotiations began. 'I'll do the outside; you do the inside' was my opening gambit. Men's work stops at the doorstep, I've always argued. Or begins if you're heading out the door. This was eventually agreed upon, and all went happy as a marriage bell, as the poet says. Until we came to the deck. We have windows opening on to the deck. I demurred at having to do the outside of these deck windows. 'The deck's got a roof,' I argued. 'Therefore it's inside. So you do both sides.' This was not a proposition favourably looked on by the fair one. Negotiations were resumed. The union mentality runs hot in my blood. I come from a long line of union organisers. My log of claims was laid out in no uncertain terms, and I claimed victory. Time for morning tea. I drank with an easy mind, while I watched the beloved working away at the outside deck windows. But wait a minute, what's that funny taste in my tea?

Rubbish Removal

In the old days, our rubbish didn't worry us. Cheerfully, we chucked everything in the one bin and that was the last we saw or thought of it. But now, rubbish is a major source of anxiety and mental breakdown. I'm not thinking of the future of the planet, not at the moment, at any rate. It's the pressure to conform to the moral force applied by society. At our place this is played out in what you might think were small ways, but to us it's a matter of extreme concern. First, we must separate out the food scraps. They go in the red bin, but what to wrap them in? Paper? That's recyclable. A plastic bag? Environmentally treasonable. We mostly use out-of-date bank statements, but we're running out of those. Next, the yellow bin. Recyclables. This involves endless discussion about what is and what isn't. Look for the little black triangle, they say. But here are two identical black plastic containers. One has a triangle, the other hasn't. We try to remember the jingle. Is it 'If in doubt, throw it out'? Or is it 'In a spin? Chuck it in'? Then there's the soft plastic. It needs a separate bag (plastic?) for the collection bin at Woolies. By now it's eleven o'clock and time for a strong cup of tea. Tea bags? Recyclable? Pass the aspirin packet. Recyclable?

The New Diary Dilemma

I have this problem every year. Everyone needs a diary, don't they! And everyone needs their new diary before the old one runs out. Of course. Here lies the problem. Let me explain. December comes round. I start making arrangements for the next year, so I need next year's diary. Now, I know it's quite probable I'll be given a new diary for Christmas. It's an appropriate present for a man, and it doesn't cost a fortune. But I need that new diary now, not at Christmas time. You see the dilemma: buy one, then receive another as a gift later on, or don't buy one and run the risk of not having one at all. Shakespeare, as ever, knew all about it. 'To buy or not to buy, that is the question,' he wrote. What usually happens is that in mid-December I buy my new diary. The next day, I'll be given one. Now comes the need to act quickly. Choose the better one, keep it, and pass the other one off to an unsuspecting male relative. Often there's a triple play. A third diary arrives. Extra speed is now needed in dispensing with the superfluous one, but being careful that it's not the original gift in case the two donors compare notes. 'O what a tangled web we weave'. Sir Walter Scott this time. I think he must have had a diary problem, too.

Past and Present

I used to teach school in the days of yore. Sometimes the old times leap back at me in surprising ways. I had a meal earlier this year with a boy I taught in Wangaratta over half a century ago. He wrote a poem when he was thirteen, and I remembered this poem, or most of it. It used to gnaw away at me that I couldn't remember it all, so I tracked down this kid, now living in Sydney, using certain covert intelligence sources I'm not at liberty to disclose. Anyway, I rang him up after this half-century lapse. I began by reading out the first two lines of his poem … and he went on with the rest of it! One thing led to another, and, hey presto, he drove down from Sydney and had lunch with me. I made another re-connection last year when Garry McDonald ('Norman Gunston'/'Mother and Son') came to Warragul to act in a play. I taught him, too, in the dim dark past. He had a beef against me, I found out. Once a week I used to eat lunch with a small group of boys at this school. Garry McDonald's beef was that I used to make them eat their meat pie with a knife and fork! Memo to all teachers: 1. Write down the kids' poems. It will save you on your phone bills later on. 2. Fingers were made before forks.

Street Talk

Now, you men, gather round and see if you don't agree. There we were, the better half and I, idling our way through the Arcade when we came across A and B (names suppressed). We hadn't seen them for fully a week. He and I, in the nature of menfolk, said hello, pressed the flesh, and walked on. But the women, who, as custom dictates, should have fallen into step behind us, were nowhere to be seen. Ten minutes, they were, nattering, while we two stood there with nothing to say to each other. Very awkward, it was. Women should be more understanding. Streets are for walking, not talking. It beats me how women develop this tendency to manufacture conversation. Using minimal raw materials, they can spin a conversation of gigantic proportions. We men know how to talk to each other. Saturday's match, how much rain we had, then, 'Be seein' ya, mate,' and we're off. We're surface skimmers, we men. You don't go round sharing the innermost with strangers. But, women! 'What were you talking about?' I mutter, when we're safe and alone again. 'Oh, this and that,' she says. 'Nothing much.' Strike a light! 'Nothing much'! And they want more women in parliament! They'll have to work an overtime shift up there in Canberra, if that happens.

Sharing

We don't do a lot of sharing these days. Not like when we were kids. We'd share our chewing gum, for instance. Maybe we'd have the first chew before we handed it on to our friend, but they'd do the same for us. Or when we were playing kick-to-kick, two of us would wax. That is, we'd have every second kick with our mate, no matter who got the ball. Or if we only had one bike between two of us, we'd maybe dink each other, or, if we were going a long way, one of us would ride a couple of hundred yards, put the bike on the side of the road and walk on, while the other one would walk to the bike, ride it up the road, and put it down, and so on. When I was five, I even shared my girlfriend with the boy who sat next to me. She didn't mind. We swapped things, too. Swapping is like sharing. We'd swap sandwiches from our school lunch. I used to swap my salad sandwiches for Johnny Green's jam sandwiches all the time. We'd swap marbles; we'd swap footy cards; we'd swap stamps. One of the big kids was a serious swapper. He finished up with a collection of goods that he sold for a fortune thirty years later. Me, I always seemed to be on the losing end of the swapping, but I would never realise it until my big brother pointed it out. Then it was too late!

Food, Glorious Food

One day I'll do a survey of our local restaurants to find out what the most popular dishes are. The problem would be with the Asian restaurants, because the meals they serve are ninety per cent the same as each other. Well, they seem that way to me. My culinary taste is not hyper-sensitive, I admit. I'm chyacked in the family for ordering sausages and mash when I go out. I believe what you order should reflect the occasion and the surroundings. So, on Saturday nights, after the football, sausages are quite in order. On 14 July, jambon beurre or quiche Lorraine are de rigueur. On 26 January, kangaroo steak. 25 April: bully beef. Well, maybe you can take this too far! My casual study of others' dining habits makes me believe that people order food according to three main principles. 1. What looks nice on the next table. 2. The price. 3. Wanting to impress the other diners at their table. As far many restaurants go, the rule seems to be that there's a direct ratio between the price of the meal and the size of the serving. The higher the price, the smaller the serve. Then there's the 'Find the potato' game. The higher the price, the more you hunt for the vegetables. (Hint: look under the meat.) My recommendation: The smaller the meal, the smaller the tip.

Second Hand

There was a time when the Council would give you two vouchers each year so you could take rubbish to the tip without having to pay. Sorry, 'transfer station', not tip. It seemed a dark day when they put an end to that system. No longer could I check out other people's offerings, those valuable pieces of scrap timber, that cracked electric jug, that see-through wicker armchair. Having seen them I realised I needed them. Transfer station, all right. Well-named. Then, unloading the trailer with my own contribution to others' transfer happiness, I'd have second thoughts about half the load, so I'd return home not much lighter than when I left. It was not easy, however, to smuggle those extra items into the shed without being seen by she who must be avoided. But then they changed the system. No more visits to the tip. Instead you piled your rubbish in front of your house and the Council came and picked it up. People complained. Unsightly streets and all that. But not me. Immediately I grasped the opportunities. As soon as a new load was deposited around town, I'd know about it straight away. Sometimes I might be beaten to the scene by a better-informed hunter and gatherer, but not often. You should see my shed now!

Baby, it's Cold Inside

In our kitchen there's a stove, a microwave oven, a dishwasher, and a refrigerator. They're the main things, anyway. Unfortunately, the refrigerator and I just don't get on. There's a school of philosophy that says it's stupid to have feelings towards inanimate objects. Those people don't know me! I've long pondered why the refrigerator and I should be so distant. It may stem from my childhood. We had no refrigerator then. We made do with a cool cupboard. The cool cupboard had no bottom. You'd look down and see the dirt under the house. Up top, it went straight through the ceiling. We'd put the butter and milk there, and eggs and cheese and things like that. One wondrous day we got a kerosene refrigerator, but it never worked properly, and that's where the genus refigeratorus and I began to drift apart. Our present refrigerator is very uncooperative. It receives items obligingly, but then refuses to give them up. It cunningly hides things away from me, though not from others. I can stand looking into that refrigerator for minutes at a time waiting for the desired object to work its way towards the front until Another Person shouts about leaving the fridge door open. Didn't have that trouble with our cool cupboard.

Little Athletics

I've seen those little kids running round the park. Their legs are pumping; their chests are stuck forward; they're half looking behind them to see who's there. You see their photos in the Gazette. I suppose it's good to develop the competitive instinct in them when they're young. It's a hard world, after all. As for me, the competitive gene seems to have missed me. I did win two shillings in a foot race once, but that was when I was five years old, and I don't think any of us understood that we were supposed to beat the others. I do have one claim to athletic fame, though. I took up walking as a young man – competitive walking, you know, like they have in the Olympics. I actually won the Victorian Walking Championship three years running. The question a lot of people ask is whether it's better to have brawn or brain. Sometimes they go together. They give Rhodes Scholarships to men and women who are fast and also smart. Maybe, as a way to de-competitise the world, we could start giving scholarships to those who haven't got either brain or brawn, to encourage them. Or else do away with scholarships altogether. Tell the kids they should just do their best, and that will be all right. No winners, therefore no losers. I think I'm on a winner there!

The Bookshelves

I started with planks of timber propped up by bricks, until influence from a certain quarter forced me to buy proper bookshelves. But they're not nearly so good. The trouble with bought bookshelves is they have plenty of room for small books, but not enough for big books. So you have to put the big books on their sides, which defeats the purpose. The planks were better. Just put another brick in to make room for the bigger books. Then, how to arrange the books? I started off doing it by size, tallest one end, shortest the other. Then I did it by colour. Red books grading to green books. Didn't work. Then by author, alphabetically. But that way my cricket books were scattered all over the place, and so were the history books. I tried men's books in one bookcase and women writers in another one. But George Eliot tripped me up. I found he was a woman. So I assumed George Meredith was a woman. Wrong again. Henry Handel Richardson ditto. So I gave that up. Now I simply use the cuckoo-in-the-nest method. When you've finished with a book, you just leave it where it is. Sooner or later it will be pushed out by the mass of other books. Under this scheme, all books eventually find their natural resting place and lie there content until finally being declared lost.

Mechanicals and Me

There are certain mysteries of modern life utterly beyond my understanding. One of these is the internal workings of ATMs. You see, I lack any glimmer of mechanical understanding. I must have been away from school the day we did Mechanics. I had a losing battle with an ATM this morning. It was one of those new ones that you can put cheques into. I approached the machine with these two shining new cheques in my hand, though not with any confidence because of my previous experiences. That was my mistake. Like dogs, they can tell when you're nervous. At least I got past the 'Enter your Pin' barrier. And I'll say this for this particular machine – it bore with me while I four times tried to put the cheques into the slot. (There are four ways to do it; hence my needing four attempts). I kept on pressing parts of the window as instructed until the ultimate rebuff occurred: 'The process has failed. Please take back your cheques.' The queue behind me was clearly becoming impatient. Besides, they were blocking the street. Nevertheless, I was not to go down without a fight. Determinedly, I did it all again – with the same result: 'The process has failed'. I ripped the cheques away and entered the Bank itself. The queue was twenty yards long!

Sorry, Wrong Address

Ah me! There are many problems to interrupt the smooth course of domestic felicity. The cat gets sick; you put the wrong bin out for collection; the washing machine stops washing. But these are temporary afflictions. There is one continuing cause of interference to our homely peace, and that is the letters that keep on arriving for the people who used to live here. Not just immediately before. Some of them go back twenty years. We could wallpaper the house with them. We could write a history of the occupation of the house. We've given up writing 'Return to Sender' on the envelopes. Now we just write, 'Grrrrr!' Do you think they'll see the point? We think of other solutions: just throw them in the bin; slip them into the neighbour's letter-box after dark; collect a couple of dozen and return them in person, demanding expenses; actually open them and see if we could blackmail the recipients (if we knew where they were); write an embarrassing love letter to the sender and/or threaten to sue them for breach-of-promise. There's one thing that stops us from taking such dire steps. It's the people who live where we used to live. They're so kind to us. They're always dropping round letters addressed to us at their place. Can't thank them enough!

Lost and Found

So K-Mart is coming to Warragul. Wow! People seem to be very happy about it, especially the Shire Council. But I have my doubts. You see, I've only ever been to one K-Mart in my life, and that was in Moe last year. I went to get a new cover for my iPad. They sell 150 000 different things at that K-Mart, and I wanted one of them. The place was as big as six Boeing aircraft hangers, and to get about you had to follow the signs up and down the aisles in an ever-expanding labyrinth. You turn one corner and another maze confronts you. At last I found an Enquiry Desk, and joined the queue which itself went around several of those corners. OK, I did get my iPad cover, I admit, though it was the next day before I escaped into daylight. At the back of my mind all the time was what happened to me when I was three years old. I was lost in Myers in Melbourne for what seemed like several days at the time, but was probably about ten minutes. When that K-Mart comes to Warragul, I fear a huge rate of child-losing. Parents and children wandering those endless aisles for eternity, looking for an exit – any exit – or maybe even the Enquiry Desk. 'Excuse me, have you any red-haired blue-eyed three-year olds?' 'Certainly Sir, just follow the signs'.

Beware of Frogs

You might see that sign in Neerim South soon. They've started an annual Frog Festival. I was reading their programme. It's held at the new wetlands below the town, and if the frogs don't turn up, you needn't worry because they're bringing in some snakes, lizards and "a diverse assortment of Aussie creatures" for the occasion. I just hope they take good care with those snakes, or there might not be any frogs there next year. There will also be 'bug adventures', which sounds dangerous. What sort of bugs? And how are they going to fence them in? Bugs have a nasty habit of being where you don't want them. All credit, however, to Neerim South for this initiative. But if Neerim South can have a Frog Festival, what else might we see? A Swamp Creature festival in Bunyip? (Loud booming sounds transmitted through the town at night-time.) A wild dog festival in Warragul? (The Council could forego registration fees for dingoes as an encouragement). A lyrebird festival for Buln Buln? (Prizes for the best imitation lyrebird in front gardens). Meanwhile, back in Neerim South, where they already have all that street sculpture, will they be having a giant concrete frog at the entrance to the town? Might scare the snakes away!

Bird Life

The closer you are into the middle of town – either in Drouin or Warragul – the more bird life there is. I put it down to the fact that there are a lot of large trees in the town centres, while in 'the suburbs' there are fewer, and in the new developments the trees haven't had time to grow (or there's no room for them!) Take Warragul. In our new house near the shops, we hear the kookaburras every morning and evening, but we never heard them when we lived further out. And the magpies. They chortle away all through the day. One came to our back door a couple of days ago and we threw it a bit of bread. Yesterday it returned. The door was open and it hopped right in, nodded briefly in our direction, flew around the room for a while, went through to the bedroom, hopped across our bed, and finished up with a ceremonial flight down the passage-way and out the front door. Made us feel like the Birdman of Alcatraz. We knew a family at Neerim years ago who found a pet magpie by the side of the road. They took it home, and discovered it was a Collingwood supporter. "Carn the Pies!" it would screech, and "Kick the b....y ball!" Showed a sound knowledge of football, that bird, and had that Collingwood look about it, too.

That's Me!

'Know thyself' commanded the Delphic Oracle, and I've been trying to do that all my life. Some say you go through a series of 'development crises' when you're young, and you don't develop unless you get through each of them successfully. Well, I had plenty of crises in my youth, and I seem to have failed them all. Is the theory wrong or am I psychologically stunted? Don't answer that question! Others say where you were born in the family is important. Well, I'm the youngest of four, so, according to the same experts, I'm "fun-loving, uncomplicated, manipulative, outgoing, attention-seeking, and self-centred". Everybody knows that experts are never more than half right, so I've cut out half of those descriptors. The three that are patently incorrect are the third, fifth, and sixth. Look around you. Are not all the youngest in their family like me – fun-loving, uncomplicated, and outgoing? Come to my next party and you'll see what I mean. Your birth-date is also important. Henry Ford and Arnold Schwarzenegger are the only other people I know who were born on my birthday. That poses a dilemma. Should I put my fun-loving, uncomplicated and outgoing personality into making cars or going into films? Add another quality – indecision!

Mowing the Lawn

One of the tests of manhood is the ability to carry out the operation known as Mowing the Lawn. This begins with starting the mower. There are two tried techniques. 1. Push it to a nearby garage and get them to start it. Leave it running while you push it home again. 2. Go to a car shop and buy a can of 'Start ya bastard'. This is guaranteed to work. Take out the spark plug (see mower operation manual), spray some of the aforesaid starter into the hole, then pull the starting cord, not forgetting to replace the spark plug beforehand (see operation manual). You are now well on the way. Carefully remove dog droppings, beer bottle tops, and clothes pegs from the lawn. Lower the cutting blades to the desired height (see operation manual), then push gently in a forward direction. Mow one strip. Call the wife to admire your work. At this point you may take a break for a cup of tea or talk to the neighbour over the fence, subtly referring to the length of his grass. The rest of the operation depends on (a) whether the mower stops running; (b) whether the forecast rain begins to fall, and (c) whether your wife's afternoon tea friends object to the noise just outside their window. (In case of any of the above, see operation manual).

The No-Train Show

We've got a lot to thank Robert Stephenson for. He was the one who built the first train. Since then, we've been able to glide smoothly to our destination, nowadays in air-conditioned comfort. Well, maybe not today. The trains aren't running today. Not on the Traralgon line. Nothing's broken down. It's just that they've got to make things better – little things like signalling and preventing head-on collisions. We're used to it, we Gippslanders. After all, we've battled things like fire and flood, Jeff Kennett, and mad cow disease for a hundred years. We're the stoic ones. Shrug the shoulders and get on with life. That's us. Excuse me, I hear someone saying. Read the letters to the papers. Come down to the station early in the morning. OK. There may be divided opinion about using buses instead of trains. And I sympathise with those who are messed around. But some are lucky. I heard of one guy they couldn't find a seat for on the last bus from Southern Cross, so they sent him home to Warragul in a taxi, free of charge. As for me, I must be one of the lucky ones also. I had an express bus trip to the City and back again, and got home before the train was due to arrive. I think that probably proves Einstein's Theory of Relativity ... or does it?

Candid Camera

Did you hear about those young hooligans who put three crocodiles into a school up at Humpty Doo? Shoved them through a window at night. Up to two metres long, they were. They saw who did it because they were filmed on CCTV camera. The police are looking for three two-metre-long hooligans. You can't do anything these days without being filmed on CCTV. I walk down the street and back and I'm filmed half a dozen times. I'm not worried about my privacy. I just want my appearance money. You can have CCTV cameras attached to your home. Great! Now I'm filmed whenever I visit next door. Or when I'm slipping something into my neighbour's rubbish bin. Or taking something out of it. Maybe I am worried about my privacy after all. Can't they invent a CCTV camera that only films bad characters? And is there a use-by date on all this film they're shooting? Have I got the right to see the footage taken of me? There might be a good shot there to use when they show those photos at my funeral. I don't think they thought of all these things when they started up this CCTV caper. Meanwhile my wife is thinking about putting a camera in the kitchen to see who's been raiding the fridge. I tell her it must be one of those crocodiles.

House of Cards

Gone are the days when folk would spend the evening sitting round playing cards. Ruined by television, then board games, and now these hand-held devices where you play against yourself. Everything has gone individual. Entertainment was a simpler matter in my young days. I remember the thrill when someone gave us a bobs set. Who plays bobs now? Euchre was a family favourite. What joy when you saw the joker and maybe the right bower in your hand! Then there's 500. It's listed as the national card game of Australia, though I'm not too sure about that. What tactics, what bluff, what teamwork, were needed there! For me, the all-time absolute best card game is six-handed 500. The only other game that took on with us was crib. People we knew were playing rummy and coon can, but not us. Whist was too easy, bridge too hard. Euchre, 500, and crib - these were our stock-in–trade. There were euchre tournaments in the supper room at the Hall while the monthly dance was going on next door. The town matrons would sit at long trestle tables in unforgiving concentration. If you won, you moved up the table. If you lost you stayed where you were. I can't understand why we don't get back to these old games. In fact, you could say I'm euchred!

Modern Postie

I must have offended the postie. He's just ridden past without leaving us a letter. That's five days in a row. And after me leaving a box of chocolates out for him last Christmas! Maybe I shouldn't be upset. The last post he left here consisted of a pizza advertisement and two letters for the previous occupants. Will posties soon be a thing of the past? People do their business on-line these days. Me too. Mostly. Though I go to the Post Office at times. Why do they still call them Post Offices? They're more like General Stores. You can buy a fold-up picnic table at the Post Office. Really! To get to the counter, they place tempting objects along the way - things like plastic teddy bears and Hawaiian place mats. It reminds me of the sirens tempting the sailors who passed by. Like Odysseus, I tie myself to the mast and walk stolidly towards the counter. Is there a use for the Post Office, then? A postal use? Yes. You can send parcels from a Post Office. You can also buy stamps there. You know, those little sticky things that go at the top corner of envelopes. Envelopes? The things you put your letters in. Those old-fashioned things for communicating with your friends. Friends? The things we used to have when we wrote letters to each other.

Bowls

I'm very ambivalent about the game of bowls. On one hand, it has a dubious background. Playing in public used to be banned in England because of the doubtful characters of the players. Then there's the little thing you aim at. Some people call it 'Jack' and others 'Kitty'. Some ambivalence there, too! Yet the game is woven into the fabric of history. Was not the noble Sir Francis Drake playing bowls on Plymouth Hoe when the Spanish Armada was sighted, and did he not finish off the game before finishing off the Spaniards? Some of my best friends play bowls. They tell me it's a great game, but then, they're biased. I look in the local paper each week to see the action photos. Most of the action seems to be bending over the ball before you send it down the green. They never show you the business end of the operation. I played bowls once. My one and only time, though I'm open to offers. I was a little put off by reading the Regulations from Bowls Victoria. It says there that players should wear head protection. Head protection? From attack by irate opponents? From a misdirected bowl? From swooping magpies? I need to be reassured about this. Meanwhile, I've had an approach from the Keenagers, that table-tennis crowd. Do I need a hard hat for that?

Shop Assistants

People who work in shops get a bad press. Take the man in 'Mulga Bill's Bicycle'. The grinning shop assistant there is not at all a nice fellow. But that's not how I've found them, these shop assistants. They're always very nice to me. Sometimes I wonder how they put up with it, being polite to people all the time. Shop assistants are mostly women, of course. Women have more patience than men, everybody knows. Some shop girls have gone right out of their way to help me. Once, at a chemist's in Warragul, they didn't have what I wanted, and a shop girl ran – ran! sprinted! – through the streets to get it from another chemist's. I watched her. She ran like the wind! For me, the best sort of shop assistants are the ones who don't bother you when you come into the store, but let you do a reconnaissance. We men don't like to be hassled. In the supermarket, the shop assistants I use most often are my fellow-shoppers. When I can't find something I turn to one of them and put on my goofy 'mere-male' attitude and ask them. They always know. And they love to help me. These incompetent males! But it's a win-win situation. They go away feeling they've done their good deed for the day, and I go away with what I came for.

The Vegetable Garden

It's time to report on my vegetable garden. It's a new garden, the first fruits in our new house. I've been bandicooting the potatoes. They emerge shyly from the cool earth, surrendering to my fatherly touch. I sent a photo round my friends, then ate them. I'm not sentimental. The carrots have been a mixed lot. You know how the seeds are so small you have to be careful not to plant them too thickly. I had this idea to mix the seed with tea leaves to help spread the seed out. It worked. The carrots have grown beautifully. But they've got a funny taste. I can't quite place it, but it reminds me of something. The leeks. They're a sad story. I didn't want to waste space so I planted them between the potatoes. Now when I dig the potatoes, the leeks come up too. Ah well, you live and learn. The radishes came up for air, took one look, then said goodbye. The cucumbers were being smothered by the tomatoes, so I transplanted them. Memo to young gardeners: never try to transplant a cucumber. The corn is as high as a wallaby's eye, and the lettuces are growing with all their heart. But the tomatoes: they're my crowning glory. Little tom thumbs clamouring to be picked. 'Thumbs down,' I say, as I slip them down the hatch.

Blood on the Floor

They were advertising this show on TV. *'Watch actual brain operation'; 'hernia removed while you watch'* or words to that effect. Not me, thanks. I don't think I'm squeamish, or not more than the next man. I'm not like that Doc Martin. I can stand a little bit of blood. Someone else's preferred. But when it comes to opening up the body to reveal unmentionable parts beneath, I'm not your man. I *have* been on the operating table once or twice. It was a breeze … when it was over. The worst part was when they stuck that needle into the back of my hand. I always look the other way at that point. My cheerful badinage suddenly dries up. My tongue sticks to the roof of my mouth. My eyes retreat into my head. I believe there's a word for it: needlephobia (noun; singular; masculine). Well, here they were on the TV spruiking this show about watching someone else's internal organs being broadcast in high definition. Actually, I had a slight onset of phobia at that stage, but my helpmate, very experienced in such situations, was on hand to administer the necessary antidote – switch off the set and utter soothing words. I'm thinking of going back to a black and white television. Colour is not always a good thing for a sensitive man like me.

Looking over the Garden

There's a regular pattern to receiving visitors at our house. 'How nice to see you,' we all say together, at the front door. Then – and now I'm warming to my subject – 'Would you like to see the garden?' Invariably the answer is yes, enthusiastically from the female party, less exuberantly from him. There follows a harrowing fifteen minutes, the women admiring every curl of every leaf and enquiring at each step whether this is a prostrate vernicular or a hairy-leaved vernicular, and recalling every species of vernicular known to humankind. The two men, meanwhile, are standing obsequiously by, longing for the cool of the kitchen and the promise therein of hot tea and scones. My particular difficulty with this routine is not just that I've been through it many times before, but I'm aware of the little evasions and half-truths coming from the lips of my fair one, who is supreme in the art of bluffing. Perhaps all women are like that. If I were running this garden tour, I'd be saying, 'This is a rose. Here's some onion weed. And this is oxalis; we brought it from our last place.' But all things come to an end, and eventually we reach the sanctuary of indoors. 'Lavender tea?' enquires the hostess. 'From our own lavender.' The men sink into silence.

Family Photos

In the old days, the husband sat, the wife stood, and the children were draped around. No smiling on any account. These days smiling is prescribed. 'Come on, smile,' they say to me. That's my trouble. I don't smile well. My best attempts come out as a sardonic grimace. I see these smiling people in the local paper. How do they do it? I go into other people's places and see row upon row of family photos on walls, bookshelves, pianos, even in the lavatory. Everybody smiling. Our place is free of such frippery. There's another factor at work. Once you get into the advanced retirement years, as I have done, you can't help thinking that every time one of the family thrusts a camera in front of you and orders you to smile, they actually have in mind the catalogue of embarrassment they plan to put on the screen at your final public appearance – in the funeral parlour. I hate to think of it. When nobody's around, I practise smiling. I practise the Giaconda smile, that enigmatic smirk on the face of Mona Lisa. I practise Hugh Grant's toothy grin. I even try a cheesy Scott Morrison 'G'day Mate' number. They all come out, however, as a cross between Graeme Kennedy and Barnaby Joyce. For me, grinners are certainly NOT winners!

The Hot Spell

Gorblimey, it was hot! So hot the bitumen melted in the main street and two old ladies got stuck in the tar. Fined for obstructing the traffic, I believe. Hot, and dry with it. You remember that heat wave in January? It was as bad as Marble Bar. Nearly lost my marbles ... and as for the bar...! My wife gave me a rain gauge for Christmas. By the end of January it had nothing in it so we took it to Bunnings and got our money back. The Celsius readings are getting more like the old Fahrenheit readings every year. They'll catch up by the end of the century, if you ask me. They tell me the Weather Bureau stopped measuring the temperature 'cos the mercury boiled over. Public behaviour changed, too. Why, in Warragul they even stopped complaining about the one-way streets. Down in Melbourne, there was so much hot air they thought Parliament must have resumed. People were ironing their clothes with the palms of their hands. In the restaurants, when people asked for a rare steak, they held it out the window on a stick for five minutes. There was so much sunburn they couldn't tell the Australian and the West Indian cricket teams apart. My mate decided to get away from it all. Went to Alice Springs. He'd heard tell it was nice out there.

ROLLICKING RHYMES

THE BATTLE OF LARDNER'S TRACK
(Have a grain of salt handy)

It was in the year of sixty-four.

Ah! Massacre and ruin!

With civil strife between the folk

Of Warragul and Drouin.

No one knows who started it,

Or who should take the blame.

A quarrel over girls, perhaps,

Or the local football game.

Drouin called up all its men;

They met in Civic Park.

Their leader was Big Bully Smith;

He was known as 'Ironbark'.

They lined up in their regiments;

Big Bully, he addressed them.

And when the cheering all was stopped,

Why, Father Murphy blessed them.

At Warragul 'twas much the same.
Three hundred men at least.
All eager to exact revenge,
Each man a savage beast.

Rockfist Logan was in charge,
A man of huge proportion.
A railway sleeper in his hand,
And a gum branch for precaution.

Each side set out to meet the foe;
They met at Lardner's Track.
Big Bully turned and faced his men,
Before the order to attack.

'Once more into the breach, dear friends';
My God! He's quoting Shakespeare!
'And once you've gained the victory,
I'll give a wagonload of beer.'

Meanwhile on the further shore,
In language mean and plain,

The Rockfist gave his orders
To smite and smite again.

He waved his massive tree-branch,
His men answered with a roar
Could be heard far off in Rokeby,
And maybe Singapore.

No less the valiant Drouin men
Engaged the mortal foe;
No quarter given; none was asked.
Would any see tomorrow?

All day long the battle rolled;
Ferocious mauls and brawling
Men of both sides proved their worth,
With many warriors falling.

And now the shades begin to fall.
A dismal scene's before us.
Our gallant Bully Smith is gone,
And Rockfist stands victorious.

The Drouin men begin to yield;
They've lost, in very truth.
But now from out their ranks there steps
A lad, a boy, a puny youth.

A stripling, he, but wiry,
Filled with gameness and with pride,
In his hand he carries river-stones,
With a shanghai by his side.

Rockfist lifts his bludgeon high:
"You fight with sticks and stones?
I'll send you now to kingdom come;
The dogs shall lick your bones.'

Our hero takes his catapult;
His eye is calm and straight.
He fires; the giant topples.
He's past all love and hate!

Now all the men of Warragul
Draw back in mortal fear.
The Drouin men rush forward
With a death-defying cheer.

The tide is turned, the field is won;
They wear the victor's crown;
Deep now they drink in victory's wells,
And history's made for Drouin town.

And there in Drouin township,
Where the pine-clad ridges rise,
When tales are told of daring feats of yore,
There's always one romance that takes the prize -

Of a lad, a sling, a river stone,
Who played a deadly game,
And a town that stood its ground that day,
And won immortal fame.

MY BIG DAY OUT
(or *'What Might have Been'*)

My big day out; you understand;

All day in town; I had it planned.

At first, by train to Flinders Street;

I'd booked, of course, a first-class seat.

A coffee next, you might suppose,

At RMB or Milky Joe's;

Then stretch my legs around the joint,

Through the Mall and Centrepoint.

Find a decent men's suppliers,

Henry Buck's or maybe Myers;

Catch the fashions; buy some jeans;

And why not me, a man of means?

Now it's time to head uphill;

A T-bone steak at the Charcoal Grill,

A cup of good old English tea,

Then catch the tram to the MCG.

The mighty Dons and the Kangaroos;

Against that crowd, how can we lose?

To keep me going, I might just take,

A pie and sauce at the half-time break.

The game is done, the flags come down;

I'll follow the crowd back into town;

A snack at Macca's next perhaps,

And now it's time for making tracks.

Platform Ten at six-fifteen,

Find my seat and all's serene;

And if by then I'm all dead-beat,

I'll go to sleep in my corner seat.

So that's the day that might have been,

My one day out; see what I mean?

So bear in mind for your next big trip,

'Twixt the cup and the lip there's many a slip.

For me, in fact, it was never to be;

The reason why, now don't you see?

That morning, I found 'twas all in vain;

Alas, poor me; I missed the train!

ABEER CATCHES THE TRAIN
(*A sorry tale of the Sub-Continent*)

On a hot and steamy morning

In nineteen eighty-four,

The rusty old steam engine

Pulls out from Bangalore.

The carriages are crowded,

The doors are opened wide;

A tangled mass of peasant folk

Is jumbled up inside.

Abeer is there among them;

He looks around the train;

A good and honest fellow,

But a man of simple brain.

He's going home to see his Mum,

He proudly tells them all,

Who's waiting there to welcome him

In the town of Madugall.

'*Madugall!*' they cry as one;
'*We've got bad news for you;*
We go express to Jalahall;
At Madugall - straight through!'

Now poor Abeer is mortified;
His hopes go up in smoke;
He doesn't care for Jalahall;
He just wants to see his folk.

But there's one man who's seated there,
Who says, '*Now I recall,*
They're working on the railway line
Just hard by Madugall.

The train goes really slowly;
It's just the break you need.
You can get off if you're careful
Before the train gains speed.'

So now the plan is settled;
Madugall is drawing near;

'Don't jump, but get off running
Or you'll crash down on your ear'.

Bravo, and now he's done it,
Abeer our hero bold;
In classic running style,
The same as he's been told.

He runs beside the carriage,
The poor old dunderhead,
And is level with the people
In the carriage just ahead.

A man at full pace by the track,
Their startled gaze reveals,
While the train is going faster
With each turning of its wheels.

'Poor man! He must not miss the train!'
They cry with one accord,
And reaching down in sympathy,
They haul him up on board!

THE RING-IN
(A tale from the early days)

This tale's as true as I'm standin' here,
But don't be taken aback
If you see my fingers doubly crossed
Firmly behind my back.

We'd had some wins and were pretty sure
We'd make the four that year,
But those brutes from Neerim North, you know,
Were on top, with space to clear.

It was then that Jigger Jones spoke up;
It was he had the bright idea;
His brother's lad in the VFA
Was killing 'em all that year.

"We'll fix him with another name,
And keep him till September;
A hundred quid will swing the deal;
Five quid from every member."

Sol Sloane, the chairman, had his doubts:
"He'll need to qualify."
But Jonesy had it all worked out:
"We'll use young Billy Bligh;

"The lad's a youngster, still at school;
We'll give him number four.
He can play until the finals start
As, let's say, William Moore."

And so the scheme was put in place
In secrecy severe;
The cash was all on Neerim North,
Unbeaten all the year.

The semi came, and North would win,
And by a country mile;
But we'd placed our bets at outside odds,
And stood by with a smile.

The team ran on to start the game,
Including number four,

Who'd got to know his team-mates
At the pub the night before.

We lost the toss and had to kick
Against the wind first quarter;
Five goals to none at quarter time
To US! It was a slaughter!

Five goals to none, and would you know,
All five by number four;
The champ, he turned 'em inside out,
While North, they failed to score.

Though we was crowin' loud and long,
Old Sol, he shook his head:
"There's somethin' goin' on out there,"
An' we looks towards their shed.

Their coach, he's got his team around;
He cries, "That number four;
I reckon he's that Jones from town;
I've seen his face before.

"They call him 'Slogger' there, you know;
We'll put him on the spot";
And he goes aside with Bully Clark,
While they hatch a little plot

No sooner had we re-commenced,
Our champ picks up the leather;
Big Bully Clark's behind him,
Just the two of them together.

"Handball, Slogger, now," he calls;
It worked a wicked treat;
Our hero turns and hands it on;
His non-de-plume is beat!

So now they know they've got their man;
His future's lookin' bleak;
Bully lines him up and sends him straight
To the middle of next week.

I hardly need to tell the rest;
Our team just chucked it in.
The Neerim boys kicked fifteen goals;
We just took it on the chin.

Now down our way when tales are told,
You'll never hear a mention
Of the day we played a ring-in cold,
And got a year's suspension.

TRAMWAY TO THE PAST

(In honour of a bygone age)

I close my eyes in reverie and let my mind run free,

And travel back to the timber days, of dray and axle-tree,

Of gallant beasts and reckless men, when none would call
it quits

As horse and man together teamed to harness Nature's
gifts.

There's a shout of 'Gee off, Brownie', and the sound of
creaking gear,

As a team of old bush horses and a load of logs appear.

The driver's old Joe Prescott from out past Drouin West;

Of all the teamsters in the bush, they call this man the
best.

The logs stacked high on bogies that ride on wooden rails

Now snake their way through bushland along half-hidden
trails.

The horses smell the curls of smoke that drift upon the
breeze,

And Joe allows himself a smile to think he soon will be at
ease.

The logs are now unloaded and I see an awesome scene;

The slip-bench slides full forward and the saw bites deep and clean.

I hear the scream as the blade drives keen, and chips fly through the air;

The men on deck can do no less than toil and sweat and swear.

There's the steady throb of the Hornsby Ten, the hiss of steam escaping;

Young Fraser works the docking bench; his back is close to breaking.

The sawdust falls to the pit below, the slabs accumulating,

And all the while a massive pile of messmate logs is waiting.

The magpie sings and the jackass brings his mirth from the branches high,

While men below work their lives away, nor ask the reason why.

They toil each day, and take their pay; that's all they need to know;

Their axes swing and the ranges ring with their cries, 'Stand by below!'

Close by, a paling cabin stands, near a trickling waterway,

Where a wife spends anxious hours and days, and children run and play,

Absorbed in their childish pleasures, confined in this lonely glen,

Strangers yet to the ways of a world that lies beyond their ken.

Yet now the vision starts to fade; I reach to touch old Joe,

But his shade of old recedes from sight in the mists of long ago.

For all those folk now fled the yoke of life's capricious hold,

With quickened heart I raise my glass to those pioneers of old.

STAN AND STATISTICS

(Stan discovers in a 2011 study that the average Australian walks 900 miles a year. Another study finds that Australians drink an average of 20 gallons of beer each year.)

We were sittin' at the bar,

Not goin' very far,

With nothin' else to do,

But sink a jar or two,

When me mate, 'e sez to me -

'e's got the paper there, ya see –

It says here, Blue, in black and white;

It's in the Sun, it must be right;

The average Aussie bloke -

It's not a flamin' joke -

Walks nine hundred mile –

I couldn't help but smile –

A year, he says. *Don't smirk;*

That's 'ere to flamin' Bourke.

Each year, it says, right here,

An' he takes a bit of beer.

Stan, he really took it in,

An' I couldn't help but grin.

But then I see 'im drop 'is jaw;

'e's gone an' found some blinkin' more.

Well, that damn beats the bloomin' lot;

'is finger's pointin' to the spot;

It reckons – it's no bleedin' lie -

That same average Aussie guy

Drinks twenty gallons o' beer

Each single blessed year;

Twenty gallons a year

Of standard Aussie beer.

I looks at 'im; 'e looks at me;

We sit all still a while, ya see;

Stan's thinkin' hard, 'is brain's alight;

'is eyes, they're big and shinin' bright.

I get this strong sensation

That 'is brain's in circulation,

When 'e jumps up on 'is feet,

An' waves the printed sheet.

Not bad, he says - 'e's standin' tall;

Not bad, he says, *not bad at all;*

Twenty gallons ... an' nine hundred mile -

You shoulda seen 'is stupid dial -
Well, blow me down, he says, *each year* -
An' still 'e grins from ear to ear –
A gallon of juice, he says, with style,
Will see me walkin' forty-five mile.
He shouts to me, *Just use ya melon;*
Forty-five mile for every gallon;
Just think of it, ya flamin' coot;
I'm doin' better than me ute!

THE BALLAD OF PADDY MURPHY

(who used his noggin, but came to the wrong conclusion)

At the Adelaide railway station

In nineteen thirty-eight,

A little scene played out that day;

The facts I'll now relate.

Some folk are not at ease with trains;

They don't like standing near.

To buy a ticket fills their heart

With anxiety and fear.

Now Murphy was as one of these;

He'd never caught a train;

The need to buy a ticket

Was an existential strain!

He had to get to Melbourne,

So much to his dismay

He faced up to the station;

He could find no other way.

He had to buy that ticket;
That much he'd heard about,
But how to go and *do* it -
That darn near knocked him out.

So he loitered by the entrance,
Now feeling rather ill,
Till he saw a box-like window
Around a narrow grille.

And above in faded letters,
Which lifted up his heart;
'TICKETS HERE', was all it said,
But he now knew where to start.

But how to go about it?
That dark and fearful grille -
What may lie behind it?
His nerves turned over still.

But Murphy wasn't lacking sense,
As everybody knew,
So he thought he'd wait till someone else
Would show him what to do.

So clever Paddy Murphy
Stood close against the wall,
His eyes and ears alerted
To catch what might befall.

And lo there came a maiden
Who said with matchless ease,
As she counted out her money,
'Alice Springs, single, please'.

She passed across some money.
Even Murphy now could pick it,
And the shape behind the window
Handed through her precious ticket.

And now there comes the climax
Of this my little story,

Of how our hero that fine day
Won fame in all its glory.

He stepped up to the window
As bold as Hercules.
Without delay, he said straightway,
'*Paddy Murphy, married, please*'!

THE SENTIMENTAL BLOKE AT THE CONCERT

(On Sunday, 25th October, 2015, the Baw Baw Trio performed a concert at Wesley of Warragul. The players were Brian Chapman (piano), Daniel Stefanski (violin), and Joan Evans (cello). They were joined by Lawrence Jacks (viola) for the final work. All these are celebrated performance artists who have performed widely in Australia and overseas. The programme consisted of Haydn's Trio in G Major, Beethoven's Trio No. 5 in D, and Brahms' Quartet in G Minor. Amongst the audience was The Sentimental Bloke...)

'Sundy afternoon,' they sez, 'doo come along;

You'll luv it sure; ya can't go wrong.'

So up we goes, me girl, Doreen, me peach –

Twen'y bucks per each! –

An' takes a seat beside this grey-beard flash ol' guy;

'e looks me up an' down and rolls 'is eye.

'How ya doin', mate,' 'e sez, so 'How'd ya be?'

Sez I right back; he wasn't gonna get on top o' me!

But in a while 'e turns and gives a stupid grin –

Fair takes me in! –

An' sez, 'The old bloke on the ivories – 'e's real top notch;

I seen 'im once before, an' 'e's the one ta watch.

''is day job's at the uni, top man an' all, ya know;

'is mate's a quack, they say; they're quite the show.

The other one – the sheila jane – she's real 'igh-bred' –

I shook me 'ead –

Ya'd blimey reckon after all they's flamin' did,

They wouldn't need this job, just t' earn another quid!

Then all goes quiet like; this geezer walks right on;

'e sez we're welcome all – an' where ta find the john.

'e opens up the door, an', blow me, in there walks -

Our eyes on stalks –

Three dudes, there was, all dressed in black from bleedin'
'ead ta toe –

They stands an' grins like Chesher cats, there, standin' in a
row.

Just standin' there they woz, and nods their scone;

We clapped just like the footy when the 'awks run on.

The doc – the young cove – gives a bow, an' moseys to 'is
chair-

Like 'e don't care-

The sheila, like 'im's up the front; - she seats 'erself with
care;

The pianner bloke's behind 'em, which I think is 'ardly fair.

There's a breathless 'ush comes over us, as all the classics say,

Then the old cove 'its the keys - Gor blimey, what a spray!

The fiddle starts in next; 'e scrapes 'is bow -

Quick, like, then slow –

'e musta twigged some'ow wot the pianner cove would do;

The chello dame; she didn't look - just bleedin' 'opped in, too.

I never 'eard such stuff, for this weren't no second best;

I tell ya straight 'n all, it soothed me savage breast.

Doreen woz dinkum 'appy, but it left me feelin' sad –

Yet kinda glad –

For it made me feel all better than I think I really am –

Like caviar an' oysters – an' I'm just bread an' jam.

The first lot finished; an' we banged our 'ands a treat;

Me mate next door, the chump, fair jumpin' in 'is seat.

Doreen – 'er eyes woz laughin'; ar, she did look super grand -

I squeezed 'er 'and -

'The fiddler cove,' she sez to me, 'ain't 'e a dainty bit';

'Ya reckon so?' I sez to 'er, an' I un'itch me mitt.

Me mate next door leans over, all proper like an' prim,

'Good show?' 'O, very nice,' I chuck it back at 'im.

I took a butcher's 'ook at all the duds and fancy gear -

No 'ayseeds 'ere –

The young cove on the fiddle gets up; sez 'e, 'There's more',

An' strike me pink, ya oughta know, it's better than before!

'Baytoven', they sez; I know I'd somewhere 'eard the name.

At any rate, I'd say he knows the blinkin' game.

I thort I'd maybe 'ire him for me next year's birthday show

If I'd the dough -

But me cobber mate beside me sez 'e's long gone underground -

'A bleedin' shame,' I sez; 'we need more of 'im around.'

We 'as 'alf time, – the intervull, accordin' to me cobber

An' I take another gander at the dudes in all their clobber.

I wouldn't giv meself a buckleys ta last in all that mob -

I ain't no nob -

Then I seen old Froggy Phillips I once worked with down the Bay;

But I think 'e couldna seen me 'cos he looked the other way.

Me girl is on me arm, an' I'm feelin' bleedin' grouse;

I coulda fought a dozen coves; I'da taken on the 'ouse!

But there's no fightin' 'ere, a' course, with all these dames an' gents -

'Twould make no sense -

It's the fine arts crowd I'm in with, and I 'olds me 'ead up 'igh;

I'm soakin' up the colture, thinkin' I might give these arts a try.

It's on agen. 'It's Brarms, ya know.' It's the know-all nong next door,

Stone the crows, the mug galah; I coulda cracked 'im on the jaw.

''Oose Brarms?' me darlin' girl, she whispers low and sweet –

She 'ad me beat -

But the ol' pianner feller upped and giv us all the guff

'bout allegro and non troppo an' such 'igh-falutin' stuff.

They'd brought another geezer; it was complicated stuff;

They musta knew what's comin,' an' three wouldn't be enough.

The four of 'em was racin', seein' 'oo could do it best –

An' blow the rest! –

The ol' bloke's lookin' daggers at the other three combined;

'e seemed ta think they's tryin' ta leave 'im fair be'ind.

An' now it's gettin' quicker the further on it goes;

Doreen is all excited an' is tappin' with 'er toes.

An' grabs me arm an' 'ugs it like she doesn't know I'm there-

I walks on air -

Then suddenly it's over an' we're standin' up ta cheer;

I'm shoutin' 'Bravo! Oncore!', though they didn't seem to 'ear.

The mob starts driftin' 'omeward, an' we're standin' there alone,

When the cove wot sat beside me comes up to chew the bone.

He sez to me, all awkward like, 'Don't get me wrong, ol' chap' –

The bleedin' sap –

'Would you join me for a coffee?' an' this dam' near knocked me out,

An' I grins at 'im an' shakes 'is 'and, an' sez to 'im, 'My shout!'

ROGER AT THE MARKET
(*How not to count your pennies*)

In days long gone this tale is set,

Before we knew of dollars, cents.

We reckoned all our worldly wealth

In pounds and shillings and, then, in pence.

We learnt the tables at the school;

The classroom echoed to the sound:

'Twelve pennies to a shilling go,

And twenty shillings to a pound'.

With this in mind I tell my tale

Of Mr and Mrs William Hart

And their boy, Roger, son and heir

Who, truth to tell, was none too smart.

The agent's truck comes out from town;

The fattened cow is in the bale.

She's loaded up, to market bound,

With Roger there, to make the sale.

Now evening falls; the truck returns
With Roger in contented mood;
The cow was sold; the question now,
Was Roger rash or was he shrewd?

His dad enquires what price she brought,
And Roger says 'I saw their tricks;
They said a pound; I told them flat,
I wanted seventeen and six.'

Through all the district round about,
This tale was told with ridicule.
The lesson we can take from this?
Why! learn your tables while at school.

THE A2 986

(After thirty years of restoration in Melbourne, the steam train, Spirit of Warragul – A2 986 – returned to the town one Saturday morning in 2017. 5000 people were there to greet it. One person seems not to have joined in the general enthusiasm).

I walked down by the station

In tranquillity and calm;

I sought some undisturbed repose

Beyond all fear of harm.

But woe is me, my day was ruined,

My fine day now all sunk.

Around the bend, the peace to end,

Came a snorting wheezing smoking *hunk* –

That roaring thumping steaming monster,

A2 986!

I sat down on the soft green grass;

I chose a quiet nook;

I smiled to think of pleasures sweet,

And opened up my book.

But woe is me, my day was ruined,

You will by now have gleaned,

For down the line, with horrid whine,

Came a huffing puffing whistling *fiend* –
That roaring thumping steaming monster,
A2 986!

I marvelled at the statue
Of our worthy Lionel Rose;
I smelt the sweet petunias,
And half prepared to doze.
But woe is me, my day was ruined -
The thing I wanted least -
For down the track, behind my back
Came a grumping, groaning, belching *beast* –
That roaring thumping steaming monster
A2 986!

I sauntered sadly to my home
In deep reflective mood.
I gave myself to bitter thoughts,
And cried in accents rude,
'Ah woe is me, my day is ruined
Beyond all fair dispute';
Just then I caught a final snort

From the horrid, loathsome, gruesome *brute* –

That roaring thumping steaming monster,

A2 986!

MY DEAR OLD TARAGO
(And make sure you pronounce it correctly!)

I've trudged the track in the great outback,

From Broome through to Bangalow;

I've hiked and biked and backed my pack,

And I've camped by the Warrego;

But the places I go, this is all I know,

Bring me back, O bring me back,

To my dear old Tarago.

I've stuck by my mate in every state

From the Barkly to Bicheno;

I've seen creeks run dry at Boggabri,

Felled the forests of Dorrigo;

But the places I go, this is all I know,

Bring me back, O bring me back,

To my dear old Tarago.

On a great sheep run – O, the tales I've spun -

In the land of the brigalow;

Worked the golden grain … and a great road train,

Where the saltbush and spinifex grow;

But the places I go, this is all I know,

Bring me back, O bring me back,

To my dear old Tarago.

I've cleared the drains on the Gippsland Plains,

Milked cows down at Buffalo;

I've stood and mourned over old Yallourn,

Washed for gold up at Omeo;

But the places I go, this is all I know,

Bring me back, O bring me back,

To my dear old Tarago.

I've been to Gentle Annie, where the Tarago sets out;

It fills the dam at Neerim South, where I've caught a dozen trout;

I've swum at Picnic Point on a boiling summer's day,

And bade the Tarago farewell where it spills into the Bay;

But where'er I go, this is all I know,

Bring me back, please bring me back,

To my dear old Tarago.

SHE'LL BE RIGHT
(*Things will be all right in the end*)

A man of many parts, they said,

My new neighbour, known as Fred,

An uninspiring sort of guy,

With shaky hand and one turned eye.

His age, well, sort of middling old,

A half-moon grin, but heart of gold.

When asked for help, by day or night -

'*No fear, matey; she'll be right.*'

The sheep were out, the fence was down;

My working mate had gone to town;

I called on Fred; 'D'ya think ya might …?'

'*No fear, matey, she'll be right.*'

The pump breaks down in that big dry;

It's dead to everything we try.

We turn to Fred, though late at night -

'*No fear, matey; she'll be right.*'

Tried some carrots – a thumping crop;

Pulled 'em day and night non-stop;

Needed help – 'Fred? - he just might ...' -

'No fear matey; she'll be right.'

That year we had the record rains

The flood washed out the bottom drains

'We need your grader, Fred, tonight' -

'No fear, matey; she'll be right.'

Now down the years that's how it went;

In warm regard our years were spent.

Fred kept himself to his own place,

And we left him to his private space;

But when we turned to him in strife,

He never failed; you'd bet your life,

His answer always, clear and bright -

'No fear, matey; she'll be right.'

One day in town I got the drill

That poor old Fred was taken ill;

They said he's in intensive care;

The news, it knocked me, fair and square.

Fred was bedrock, here for good,

A fixture of the neighbourhood.

We'd come to love his cheerful sight
And '*No fear, matey; she'll be right.*'

The nurse was pleased that I could stay
To sit with Fred on that last day.
He wakened for a little while;
He held my hand and tried to smile;
He moved his lips; his grasp grew weak,
But the words came clear – the last he'd speak,
As he turned to me in the fading light -
'*No fear, matey; she'll be right.*'

Last Leaves from Uncle Jim's Diary

Over two years I have written and published more than two hundred reflections on local life, each one fitting into exactly one page of text. How I wish life was so tidy. But it is in our untidiness that we find our humanity. What do they say? Life is what happens while you're waiting for something to happen. If no one has said it before, then I claim it. After all these revelations about *your* lives, I expect you now know a good deal about *mine*! I'm sure there's a lot left to say about you, but I doubt there's much more for you to discover about me. There may, however, be something new in my poems, which I have put out for public consumption for the first time. Robert Burton long ago declared that all poets are mad. I'd re-state that. Anyone who writes a poem is a little bit mad; if they publish their poem they're definitely mad. That's a good note to end on. If you don't hear from me again, think of me shut up in some subterranean mad-house feverishly penning what no one will ever read. But Shakespeare, as ever, can have the last word. 'All the world's a stage,' he wrote, 'and all the men and women merely players.' I need to re-state that, too. 'All the world's a stage … and my direction is Exit'.